daug

Recent titles from the Cleveland State University Poetry Center:

The Hartford Book by Samuel Amadon
Rust or Go Missing by Lily Brown
The Grief Performance by Emily Kendal Frey
My Fault by Leora Fridman
Stop Wanting by Lizzie Harris
Vow by Rebecca Hazelton
A Bestiary by Lily Hoang
The Tulip-Flame by Chloe Honum
Render / An Apocalypse by Rebecca Gayle Howell
A Boot's a Boot by Lesle Lewis
Say So by Dora Malech
50 Water Dreams by Siwar Masannat
Mule by Shane McCrae
The Bees Make Money in the Lion by Lo Kwa Mei-en
Residuum by Martin Rock
Festival by Broc Rossell
The Firestorm by Zach Savich
Mother Was a Tragic Girl by Sandra Simonds
I Live in a Hut by S.E. Smith
I Burned at the Feast: Selected Poems of Arseny Tarkovsky translated by Philip Metres
    and Dimitri Psurtsev
Bottle the Bottles the Bottles the Bottles by Lee Upton
Adventures in the Lost Interiors of America by William D. Waltz
Uncanny Valley by Jon Woodward
You Are Not Dead by Wendy Xu

For a complete list of titles please visit
www.csupoetrycenter.com

daughterrarium

Sheila McMullin

Cleveland State University Poetry Center
Cleveland, Ohio

Copyright © 2017 by Sheila McMullin

ISBN 978-0-9963167-5-0

First edition

21   20   19   18   17   5   4   3   2

This book is published by the Cleveland State University Poetry Center,
2121 Euclid Avenue, Cleveland, Ohio 44115-2214
www.csupoetrycenter.com and is distributed by
SPD / Small Press Distribution, Inc. www.spdbooks.org.

Cover image: Sheila McMullin
Cover design: Amy Freels
daughterrarium was designed and typeset by Amy Freels in Garamond.

A catalog record for this title is available from the Library of Congress.

To my mother & father for teaching me how to plant.
To my ancestors for teaching me how to tend.

Table of Contents

Tapering   1

Bad Woman, thought drawer variation   3

Firelight Meditation   13

daughterrariums   19

Antumbra   24

Toward Myself   26

Bad Woman, gold point variation   28

Nest Hide   29

Firelight Meditation   31

Bad Woman, planning someone's falling variation   37

Bad Woman, in the beginning variation   39

Bad Woman, beneath vision seaweed variation   40

Bad Woman, reverse ghost variation   41

Bad Woman, even poppies variation   42

Like Water   43

Firelight Meditation   45

Ruth's Book   83

Olga's Book   85

Judith's Book   86

Clara's Book   90

Lilith's Book   91

Bad Woman, although ocean bottles variation   93

Crosses   94

Bad Woman, chronicle variation   95

Roadside Trash   96

Bad Woman, broken ballad variation   97

Bad Woman, lineal question variation   98

Notes   101
Acknowledgements   102
About The Author   104

Tapering

The day woke with a (*)
not a star, but a satellite

We drove through New Mexico, yes

We saw adobe cliff dwellings, no

We were leaving home, yes

Someone was running away, sure

Then you, my mother, told me, an (I),
while driving:

When I was in my twenties
I thought if there was a gun around
I might have held it toward myself

Then my mother, the you, said:

My sister also said *
we think because of our mother; (I)
feared * and (I) held *

(I) interrupted *:

Many people have that thought, sure
around dangerous objects, yes

(I) looked out the window, no

like killing myself had never come
into my own before, no
My tongue dried with half the pill

Bad Woman, thought drawer variation

A boy sticks his dick in her ass and then in her vagina.
A few days later her skin burns
and rises to 105 degrees.

Sitting in the shower's tub; blink,
waterfalls over her lips; blink,
her fingers on her eyes; blink,
ears booming like cathedral bells; blink,
her toes prune; blink.
A towel to dry off.

The concerned mother forces a hairbrush through her daughter's hair.
The daughter's scalp, like clay, molds forward then back.
Her eyebrows rise upward then down.
The corner of her lips tilt toward her ears then frown.
The daughter, wrapped in a towel cross-legged
on the mother's bed, notices that it hurts.
The mother is only trying to help.
Knots gather at the end of her hair—little fishing nets.

The mother buckles her daughter
into the passenger seat, drives to the hospital.

•

It's easier for them to shoot you
if you're up in a tree
she was told
never climb higher while under fire, keep low—
hide behind cars or big boulders, telephone booths.

And the daughter. The daughter
taciturn by the advice
to run for cover, the thought that someone
would try to kill her

is a thought—
I did not create—
I didn't create it—is a thought, I did not—
it is a thought, to create, I did not create—
is a thought I did not create it.

•

The night the daughter lies
in the hospital bed
with a narcotic in the IV
and the IV hooked into her arm,
the boy vomits onto his shoes
at a distant house party.

Doctor says,
I'm going to ask you some personal questions.
Is it okay that your mother is here?
Okay, have you ever used drugs? Blink.

·

You know dust devils in the desert?
Those aren't devils at all.
Those are ghosts, stomping their feet
to beating drums, wailing
with their arms to the sun.

·

Then, with a big palm toward the beige pocked ceiling
the mother is motioned to leave
the hospital room. The daughter is asked:
Do you use drugs?
A deep breath.

Doctor says,
Make sure to wipe yourself from front to back.
Vagina to anus. Not the other way around.

The mother, after a cue from Doctor,
sits back down in the hospital room,
says, I don't know what you told them but
what's kept in these files…
They're not private in the way they make it seem…
I mean, they're confidential, but.
The concerned mother says,
they need certain information
to treat you. I shouldn't have left.

You're a good girl.
You're still so hot.
It's my right as your mother.
These files, they categorize you out of context.
Just be careful.

The concerned mother, tired and worried,
hasn't eaten anything
the entire day the daughter lies in the hospital bed
with a narcotic in the IV
and the IV hooked into her arm.
Nurse brings in a slice of carrot cake in a plastic container.
On top a taped note written with big curly *o*'s,
For Mom.

•

The putrid smell
of the devil's tongue flower hangs like fever
in a white planter against the sunlight
through the window.

•

I know how to wipe my ass.

•

Between sapping limbs
of plum and bark
a child breaks
the skin of her hands.

Stopping the blood with sap,
she licks off her fingers what she thinks
will taste like honey.

It tastes like sick and bedtime.

•

I have seen many dead people
in my head
I have seen them at lunch and in parking lots
in my head
I have told them my best secrets and asked them for forgiveness
I believe
Paradise began in a plum tree with oak
knives mounted like stalagmites.

•

There are those who have hurt you
not because you are ignorant,
but because you have a heart.

The sky becomes skeleton
and here is your moment
          with cup in hand.

How not to blame the heart?

●

Sap still sticks to my fingers.
When the gun came into my life
there were no flying bullets, no fire, no riots,
but a barrel pointed toward my chest.

A man much larger than me
said to put my hands above my head
and empty my pockets; this at the same time.

●

Blame yourself
          with cup in hand
          while the sky becomes skeleton.

•

Even with everyone's voices in my head
Weren't you so scared? Be more careful. Be grateful it wasn't worse
do I truly believe the daughter
could have handled the situation better?

I do.

•

How not to blame myself
for being fragile?
Although she was warned,
where were the boulders or cars?
Or the telephone booths
to hide behind?
She got down low,
did as she was told,
said sorry for the things I did wrong.
I practiced cleanliness and safety first.

When they came, I was unprepared
and they took me away from myself.

There was no disaster, just incident.

How was I so unprepared?

Throw away the flower,
the planter, the window, and the sunlight behind it.

•

She wonders what he had for dinner.
I could have been a hero.
What high school he went to.
She could have refused to get down.
His birthday.
She could have fought for her things.
I could have.

I fold replays like napkins
and slide them into a drawer like my throat.
In the drawer like my wrist, a black rotary telephone.

"Hello?"

I open the cabinet like my knee,
find carrot cake and medical charts.
In the drawer like my hip, a glare off his white tennis shoes.
In the drawer like my chest, a man under a street lamp.
I open the drawer like my wrist and unfold a napkin.
In the drawer like my belly, sap.

For a long period all I could write was
Seriously?
Seriously?
With a big question mark
over and over

on a pad of yellow legal paper.

She feels her skin itching into fever.
It makes pins in the hinge of my jaw, her ears pop.

Being unprepared meant handing over her body,
but seeing as it's still attached to me
I can't let go.

●

The inside of my ears:
echoes and cathedral bells.
The difference between what you say I know
and how I feel.

Where senses intersect, and I taste what I hear.
The urge to lie and say I've grown so much.
Seeing it fall out of my mouth.

What keeps us?
Our senses. A forced rhythm.
Constant falling chests.
Breathing?
Then I am
swallowing bile back.

Closing cabinets to block the refrain.
He told me to get on the ground.
I heard the doctor telling me how to wipe my ass.

The sky above our heads
is not pocked with orange poppies
and firelight ranunculus

my heart

a plastic bag
inside many other plastic bags

In my fantasies
I sit in front of a bowl of poppies
at the kitchen table, thinking about God,
folding and refolding a napkin
in front of my face

On the corners of our lips
there is a King of May

In his pockets he holds keys
that will unlock every door
which will reap a harvest

The King does not know my name
He does not care to learn

To get access to those doors
I will have to steal his keys

If I get caught . . .

think about what he could do
This is when I feel the most fear

daughterrariums

KNOCK, KNOCK.

Knowing what will happen at the end. At the end of night, at the end of the morning, in disguise, in disgust, in a gust of wind—repulse her, own her, owner, theft, this heat. Let the sun rise over, let the candle drip on her, let you go. Let her up, give you yourself to the roadside trash, her knees bleed, let rocks, your skin, let rocks fill in like disease. Name the rocks disease, cut them out, keep in a jar, bounce the rocks like crickets, glow the crickets like fever, let them break the glass, let them fall to the ground, let the ground swallow growth, make growth swallow the air.

Act II

Who's There?

Lying side by side a lowered forearm rests between his breasts on his breast bone; I feel his heartbeats then remember my own—I am warm and getting warmer and seasick. I cup a hand around his. A thumb on his veiny wrist echoes my sonar pulsing. Simultaneous heartbeats sound: then off, the same, then off, same, off, same, off. Emerging fever, my skin, a spiraling system in pores. I listen to crickets outside and hear hundreds of them, maybe a few. Trying to pick out one I can't hear it individually. I can't sound the alarms for the lions to bulldoze the scenery. Please, dear reader, take me out of this bed and put me back in the grass.

ACT III

KNOT.

Replace *I* with daughter. Replace *hear* with moss. Exchange *singular* with lioness and redact *lioness*; insert crickets. Extinguish *if* with then and *here* with something that is equal to. Let the quiet settle in the backyard between window and fence. Then let crickets know of the daughter to end the story. Therefore, remove *start*. Make it end. Leave the smallness. Leave the statement a question. Replace *moss* with glass. Replace *glass* with daughter. Replace *daughter* with glass.

(But I couldn't hear one that sounded singular, and if here is where we start—above smallness—over the earth—is the quiet to join in the cacophony?)

Act IV

Knot Who?

With blood and black stripes all over. She began her first cycle. Felt like wet sand caught in the crotch of her bathing suit when she was younger and at the beach. Chunky and gooey and rose is a rose is a rose is a rose-colored. The daughter showed her mother. For a moment she couldn't realize what it was. The mother smelt it. Yes, you could have babies now. But don't until you have a good job. You're doing a good job now. You did the right thing telling me. Mark the phase of the moon on your calendar. Vitamin C can help if you bleed too heavy. It will be good to remember that.

Act V

Knot the Thing Noticed.

Knowing how this would begin—the lion would end up as the human child I saw in my dream as I was making up the dream while asleep lying with my arm on his chest. My dream mind chirping stories as if I were a conductor of the cacophony and would remember the pen and paper next to the bed. Perhaps pick up the sheet and write with eyes still closed, convulsing between heartbeats. Move my tongue off the top of this roof. If only this entire house were a mouth I could finally be Jonah. Dear body. Saliva slowly degrading me, drilling nutrients out of me. Finally write that down.

Antumbra

bulbs in blue glass cages.family who prays before sleep.father who
cannot see through an eye.mother who grinds black teeth.daughter.cloak
an unknown ceiling through [   ] prayer.who never

> [battlefield]
> # [waking]
> [eyetooth]

heard.devil over the shoulder glances.the who that takes a prayer.breath

> [summer wind]

like [   ].crescent umbra and full brightness everywhere, he heard.

> [chameleon paper]

to be like a mother, he heard.he heard, powdered teeth would be a fine substitute for
a [   ].wine from well buckets.salted tongue to taste what splits.

> ## [desert rind]
> [penumbra bed]
> ## [heated spine]

> [a heart into a stump]
> [believes; which is her moon]

to nightmare on the first of the month.the wind that rushes [   ]

> [washes the deer away]
> ## [only a green apple]
> [increases blood cell count]

before the night is over.mistaken lampposts for moonspots.the always know
name.would she have been a fist.unfold leaf by petal, petal by page.page
through sight.grow the shining know name.over bent knees.no broken

hearts.just a [   ].let me use alchemy.change this baby to gold.
    [tired morning song]
    [turning over and over]

Toward Myself

and I was dead too, dead when she first held me
my father was dead and buried us beneath violets
we woke up
    dear body,
I was born the son of a prince
sir of the lake
daughter of a fish and one sun ray
baptized in the juniper mash

God took our feet
  we gave praise
    we gave thanks
      asked for forgiveness
        then for the things we wanted

God took our hands
  we gave praise
    we gave thanks
      asked for forgiveness
        then for the things we wanted

a growth formed inside us
  we gave praise
purple and bulbous
  we gave thanks
a pain spongy and tissue
    dear body,
bent knees in water
    asking for forgiveness

we can place our fingers on it
we cannot remove or birth it

       then for the things I want
heavens all keep me
inside caves drunk

on that first footprint
on my love
my love on
gravity melting me
dear body, to collect toward myself again

Bad Woman, gold point variation

Imagine yourself a spectator
and a woman in a business suit walks
toward the water, keeps walking, walks.

Point to yellow and say, *This.*
This is what I've been trying to say.
Gold into water.

Imagine yourself alchemical.
Toward the water, keep walking.
The meaning of a white walleye

belly up in the river.
The meaning of a fish
not eaten alive before expiring.

The meaning of an expired body.
The meaning of floating with lungs open
to the sun.

Nest Hide

don't think voice come he touched don't think fear of falling i touched don't think i didn't touch they touched me don't think my tongue let off my teeth the roof don't think inside teeth alone through a group through a group of men alone they looked don't think he at me i looked i didn't look i needed hated want to into the i wanted to frighten am frightened the group a person in front behind me the same person to stand this still done to me i wanted to say sorry i want to wait i wanted to be absolved say forgive i want to give i wanted myself to a heavy person in these arms a person in heavy wrapping arms i didn't touch my body i didn't i walked away i took to don't think come anyway nest hide voice fear of falling

Do you fear
or have you feared
your body
because you love
your body and your
entire life were shamed for being so loving?

Because loving means you feel comfortable alone
and no one has ever left your body alone

Does regret fill
or has regret filled
every empty space?
Not just in your body
but in the fields of your mind
that extend past your skin
and into the room surrounding you?

Do you ever fear
you will always be clawing
at the angry knot twisting out of this pit?

I do

Bad Woman, planning someone's falling variation

A person lies next to me

Someone's arm wraps tenderly around my waist
So sweetly this fingertip circles my hipbone

I know this person's name

An owl circling the chimney
Eyes like brick

Eating the songbird

I forget this arm has fingers
When I say I can hear two

eyes opening and closing

I mean are they looking at me
both heads on gray pillows

one nose toward one ear one nose toward one ceiling

I am not planning on falling asleep
when the plan was to fall asleep

Angry that this is all that is left in the dark

Sleep when I'd rather escape head first
through the window the bed is facing

through glass and metal and plastic onto the grass

Are you blinking
Yes

What are you thinking about

Things I don't know
The bed makes a crunching as I turn my back to the voice

I thought the dove coos

were owls in the daytime
owls in holes in trees wide awake

whenever someone could hear them yelling

Bad Woman, in the beginning variation

Forever over the hell and call it earth, call it sunshine
God was in the movement and in the helmets

The gift that is equal to
Over our belly over the earth

Bad Woman, beneath vision seaweed variation

then bloomed the bluebells
the flowers wilted
and petals through rot
removed themselves from air
from molecules
from positives and negatives
and negatives followed a line
dedicated to what some would call
fairy path, others would call hell,
others would still call a cold wind,
until the negatives landed, found
their way to water
some lakes, some oceans, some rivers
they are all beautiful
women's faces beneath water
sucking in water
whether waves or foam
drinking in water, filling their bellies
until they become full with water
breaking the surface for breath
just above the watertop their lips puckering
dragonflies landing on a lip then flying away
dragonfly landed on a lip then flew away
arms becoming seaweed
then seaweed becoming arms again.

(first doorway then run then cave)

Bad Woman, reverse ghost variation

Olga, oh olgy olga, there are far too many people
In the world to love you and only you

Bad Woman, even poppies variation

80 million stories

Aunt Clara in her habit is 105 years old

Burns sugar incessantly

Chicken skin in her blood

Like Water

Thyme, garlic, and rosemary sprigs boil in water. Mint leaves float on rounded aureoles. Twirls of steam hobble in the kitchen and fog the green sea glass tiles. *Tiles*, one of the first words his granddaughter learned to write in cursive. "Mija, come here. Come massage your hands in this steam. Mija."

He hears the etched squawk of chair legs push against tiles. A magnetic shuffle of slippers toward him. "Your hands over this."

Open palms parallel to electric burners, her hands intended for inspection. Moisture and spice crawl through the dried creeks of her chapped skin.

The grandfather, between indexes and thumbs, lifts her hair up, holds still, lets the hair fall like water eclipsing the view of her face. He tilts her veiled face closer to the boiling pot. She feels the steam hold close to her. "Your hands can't be used as axes, mija. Your hands are resurrections." Centimeter by centimeter he urges her into the steam and wild mirror surface.

"In there, you can become an owl. Bring back the women we have lost. Do you remember when I danced around the May Pole in Mexico, when I was a boy? Mother told me to dance with a girl. In her hair I placed a marigold."

He needs me to be an owl—speak to the women who have died. Place mint on the front of our door and on my tongue. Watch for them. Raise them home.

There are elements of feeling angry
about what I feel ashamed about

I think
the anger came first

I was angry and I was shamed for being angry
Then my way of expressing anger became to feel ashamed

How do you inhabit anger
and thick saliva and hangnails?
Do you realize it?
Feel it?
Are it?

Does it depend on your body?

For me I realized

I realized I was angry
and I realized late

It was like
that time at Halloween
We were at the bar
I heard screaming
A movie was playing
There was a man simultaneously
raping and murdering a woman under a sheet

Before I would crawl into myself
or would know not to look

But this time
I didn't know
This time
I clawed at the screen
and it felt good

In the untethering of shame
I cannot stop thinking of how angry I am
and this thinking makes me furious

I demand apologies
from every family member
friend
stranger
who got in my way

in my head
I am demanding that people
deal with this angry woman
in my head

Sitting and stirring

I do not know how to be angry

I hear it the fury
And I feel violent

I feel optionless and forced to keep my body on
Invited into the fury to be drowned by guilt

I don't want to be violent

Like my throat clogged with so many fists
A fissure from my sternum to navel
a knot kneaded outward growing in waves of bile and heat
into tight cylinders of flesh at my sides sent
floating into the air from a gentle puff of breath

My vision tunnels
Everything turns green
Roaring static

My ability to make reasonable decisions
to be loved by God and earth
have been questioned

I have been made
to think I am broken and disgusting

Others took joy out of my body
when I did not

A mouth full of warm saliva

Do I deserve this?

Have I been clawing my whole life?

Never taught to be angry
without shame?

I have been told I do not deserve my anger

Do you deserve my anger?

Maybe—probably not
but there is kindling everywhere

Have I been unintentionally cruel?

Did I never realize it?

This makes me feel ashamed

An overextended body

Do you believe me?

The life being built around me
looks nothing like the heart inside of my heart

Guilt coerces me into silence

What will grow
in the untouchable space
in my throat?

The internet tells me to do something about it
My allies tell me to do something about it
Commercials tell me to do something about it
Preferably buy something about it

I was born into owing something
I am filled with things

Am I not doing something about it?

Every day I get up and am still alive

Trust me with my body

I work toward an anger that moves forward

Maybe it is quiet but it's not silent
Maybe it is getting louder

I often still feel like a very bad person
But it is getting easier to identify who is actually saying that

Gods are in my movements

You don't have to support me
You have to get out of the way

The sky above our heads
is pocked with orange poppies
and firelight ranunculus

God's hand over our belly over the earth

Ruth's Book

Previous Pap exams had come up abnormal.
Cervical cancer diagnosis in late 20's.

Ruth's doctor: ...higher rates of breast cancer in Anglos, and
Latinas get cervical cancer.

Why?

Because. Well, Anglos tend to smoke more and Latinas, well,
tend to have sex earlier and with multiple partners.

So this is why I got cancer.
Yes, he said.

        contemplating flower petals
        emmis is truth
        I was treated with the sunlight   80 million stories
        uniting spaceship earth   Aunt Clara in her habit is
        fucking derelict   105 years old
                                      Burns sugar incessantly
                                        Chicken skin in her blood

Forever over the hell and call it earth, call it sunshine.
God was in the movement and in the helmets.

                    said, I don't want to talk to you.
                    first had sex when I was 18.
        He said yes.   only had sex with two people.
                    been married 12 years.

before that we were dating for 6 years.
told me it was an infection.
told me it was an infection again.

Olga, oh olgy olga, there are far too many people
In the world to love you and only you

this passage that the gift is equal to
God's hand over our belly over the earth

Olga's Book

"In dark house" "he sees a young" "ghost girl"
"he blames me" "for" "not having pregnancies"
 "he said, well, you" "know what he"
"said," "he said," "no one" "loves" "me, like"
 "like the" "Ghost steals all the" "love"
"ghost heart" "isn't big enough" "big enough"
"love doesn't" "fill" "this house" "Ghost said"
"in ghost house" " not big enough" "Ghost said"
"'there are too" "too" "many people" "in this world"
 "to love" "you and only you'" "in this world" "to love me"
"feet never" "took" "root like"
"Ghost just" "cut them off" "Ghost" "has"
"never collected any-" "thing just my"
"things" "Ghost took" "and counted over" "and over"
"pressed violets and" "violets into" "pages of library"
"books" "ripped pages from spines"
"wrote Ghost name" "on" "the violet" "stain"
 "Ghost will have" "to bless me"
"bless me" "re-" "verse" "me" "I"
"dare you to" "uninvite me" "I"
"dare you to" "uncome in me"

God's hand over our belly over the earth

Judith's Book

Sounds she collects after surgery: Footsteps down a corridor
Turn signals
Clicking keyboard keys
Hungry stomachs
Refrigerator motors
Cat jumping onto the windowsill

Coil of lavender synapses reemerge as plastic and wire.

Before surgery objectives: What is whiter than
to buy a pen and lotion that smells nice
What is better than
some gauze too
What is rounder than
to swipe and sign for her credit card

A moment for memory and incision through the earlobe.

Incisions all around her: Register at the front desk and consent
Put pen in purse and purse to family
Quick prayer and joke
Sounds rehearsed and memory of this before
Unclothe and wash and robe
Battlefield prayer

To replace the connection that carries company into sound, and
sound into snow.

Timeline of the operation: 3:00 pm wash
3:05 pm lie in bed
3:10 pm fall asleep
3:10 pm fall asleep
3:10 pm fall asleep
thh-uh-reetin pea-m

this passage that the gift is equal to

Answer my questions 3:

Trust your nervous system.

milk and extraordinarily long long legs.
tinkering clunks and red red plums.
electrode bombast.
auditory nervousness.
lying. a suctioning kneading.
hands. my hair. the sea. my belly.
violets and violets. with sunlight.
scorched by sunlight. I am
treated with sunlight.
hand over the earth.

I will shut it down temporarily.

What is whiter than the snow
What is good and red and gold
Do I wish to be from your company

                    What is whiter than the snow
                    What is good and red and gold
                    Do I wish to be from your company

What is whiter than the snow   whiter than the snow
What is good and red and gold   and gold
Do I wish to be from your company   from your company

       What is the snow What is good and red and gold
       gold and whiter than the snow
       Do I wish to be from your company

     What is whiter than the Do I wish to be from your company
     Do I wish to be from the snow What is good and red and gold
     What is whiter than whiter than the snow
     than the What is good and red and gold and gold and red and gold
     Do I wish to be from I wish to be from

What is whiter than the snow
What is good and red and gold
Do I wish to be from your company

                    What is whiter than the snow
                    What is good and red and gold
                    Do I wish to be from your company

Clara's Book

this (that) came into me by way of God
you (God) delved straight in and
God (she) took hold, made me hurt
made me (him) shuffle our way of looking
to take that (this) into me (her)
an extreme of chamomile or vitamin C
cinnamon, an extreme of mint
I (God) once touched the leaves of a mimosa
it (he) snapped together like a mouth
held his (her) breath then
relaxed into its (God's) fern
so tiny, these leaves, I (it) thought
it's not hard to understand why
you (they) would be so scared of God (them)
easier to see how (when) he (it) does
not protect you, mimosa
burn when I (you) squat, burning sage
loosen when you (I) bleed, roasting rosemary

(listen: first doorway then run then cave) this passage that the gift is equal to
God's hand over our belly over the earth

Lilith's Book

When I sleep
I am a bad woman.

If some unfortunate
event, I think, were to rip
me out of the house and into
the street in the middle of night
my body would melt
under the eyes of the neighbors.

They would see my black,
sheer panties,
the outlined curve rounding above
my hips against the flames of the fire or whatever,
knowing no one was in the house
with me, goose bumps betraying my skin,
a forearm crushing
my breasts flat and yet, there's the cleavage.

Out there, I could step like a pearl
or pink oyster tongue.

Chips of glowing breeze
over a febrile body.

A constellation.

Let it burn.

Mirrors and poppies.

The should-be-shamed
naked woman
vesper, rebuilding her own house.

My body, blue rosemary cloak, blooming ocean.

Bad Woman, although ocean bottles variation

I found a needle in the carpet and finally asked who he had been
sleeping with. Because of this I bled.

Eating ripe tomatoes off the vine.
Juice down slides of my mouth. Skin on my teeth.

I touched the river
and men sitting on a stone wall snapped their fingers, oscillated their
arms from the elbows above their heads and yelled things toward the
river. Empty bottles sat next to each of them.

Under my foot in the
ocean, like glass, I step on and hold there some sort of fish. I was
surprised he was larger than my foot and although I felt fear I let the
wave crash.

Crosses

We only know from the ground that we shake. Or a traffic of blooming light over Alaskan Cypress. Then, we can't see past thousands of miles of dim light. The disc disappears to, what we can only guess, return home to a spouse, perhaps, share a meal. Why Earth seems brighter although we die. When babes ate their way out of fathers' heads. A man with many heavy bags prays and crosses himself the entire length of his trip.

Bad Woman, chronicle variation

When babes ate their way out of fathers' heads.

He said yes.

Roadside Trash

I have mistaken:

coyotes[1]

dogwood flowers[2]

moon spots through passenger seat windows[3]

an arm in a sweater[4]

autumn leaves singed with early winter[5]

timorous squirrels[6]

hunched workers with giant orange plastic trash bags[7]

a baby, a doll, not wanting to think that[8]

death coming for my turn[9]

deer's isosceles-knee cut away from her body darkened with asphalt, her rigamortis head taut[10]

---

1. Twisted and stained cardboard boxes on exit ramps
2. Wadded and sodden table napkins
3. Over-exposed lamp posts
4. Freezer insulation foam bulging through cement medians
5. Lines of crushed coke cans cluttering hill bases
6. Plastic pink polka dot rain boots
7. Avoidance hazard cones on off-ramp exit
8. Bundles of tattered cloth with lace
9. Speeding cars
10. Exactly that

Bad Woman, broken ballad variation

contemplating flower petals
emmis is truth
I was treated with the sunlight
uniting spaceship earth
fucking derelict

What is whiter than the snow
What is good and red and gold
Do I wish to be from your company

Bad Woman, lineal question variation

When I sleep you are in the scene.
You are white light behind the scene.

You have always been me
and I ask a different question about love.

Through the corners I exist as object
of direction, as disembodied perspective.

You were involved in my birth
though I do not know your name,

I did not know you knew my name.
I am a daughter of lineage.

Stitch patches of water along me.
Bloom a ginger flower.

The green ginger root wrapped in plastic
is only doing what it has done before.

I put the ginger flower into my mouth.
Orchards bloom inside me.

Notes

"Ruth's Book" comes in part from Dr. Juliet McMullin's interview with Ruth (pseudonym) in "Experiencing Diagnosis: Views from Latina Cervical Cancer Patients" in *Confronting Cancer: Metaphors, Advocacy and Anthropology*. Juliet McMullin and Diane Weiner (eds). Santa Fe, NM: School for Advanced Research Press. 2009 Pp.63–82.

The form within "Olga's Book" is modeled after Alice Notely's *The Descent of Alette*.

"daughterrariums, Act IV" borrows "rose is a rose is a rose is a rose" from Gertrude Stein.

"Nest Hide" borrows its title, "fear of falling," and "don't think" from a sketch by Ellen Forney in *Marbles: Mania, Depression, Michelangelo, + me*.

Bad Woman, broken ballad and parts of *Judith's Book* are inspired by the folk ballad "Riddles Wisely Expounded" (Child Ballad #1)

Mention of the King of May is both inspired by Allen Ginsberg and not at all in reference to.

Acknowledgments

Thank you Daniel Borzutzky, Caryl Pagel, and everyone at the Cleveland State University Poetry Center for your excitement about this book and bringing it to print.

Thank you Eric Pankey, again and again, for your mentorship, friendship, and constant encouragement.

Thank you Todd Fredson for being my first poetry family. Thank you Sarah Vap for showing me the brave way to cut. Thank you Richael Faithful for your compassionate attention to my spiritual wellbeing and healing. Thank you to Joan Kane, Lynn Melnick, and Sheila Black for giving me so much of your time and generously offering crucial feedback on my manuscript.

To my professors Susan Tichy, Peggy Yocom, Jen Atkinson, Sally Keith, my colleagues and peers, and Bill Miller at George Mason University where the seed of this work was planted, thank you.

Thank you to my friends for all the ways you've shown me love and support: Jennie Tal Williams, Sheryl Rivett, Courtney Sexton, John Dwyer, Rosebud Ben-Oni, Kathy Crutcher, Amy King, Rob Casper, Q Wang, Lauren Stahl, Anya Creightney, Dean C. Robertson, Sally Ball, Molly Gaudry, Jen Fitzgerald.

Thank you Mom and Dad for all those things I never said thank you for, which helped me get here today.

Thank you to my grandfather, Jesse. And especially, thank you to my love, Eric Tunell, for walking through this with me. I am grateful.

Deep appreciation to the following journals for debuting earlier versions of my poems in print or online: *1913: A Journal of Forms, A Bad Penny Review, Boog City, Counterexample Poetics: Assemblage of Experimental Artistry, The Doctor*

T.J. Eckleburg Review, NAILED, Quail Bell Magazine, ROAR Magazine: A Journal of the Literary Arts, Yew: A Journal of Innovative Writing & Images by Women.

Thank you to the following presses for seeing early promise in my work by honoring *daughterrarium* (full-length and chapbook versions) with finalist or semi-finalist mentions: Ahsahta Press, Black Lawrence, New Delta Review, Tarpaulin Sky, Two Sylvias Press, Washington Writers Publishing House, and YesYes.

About The Author

Sheila McMullin is a poet, intersectional feminist, youth ally, and organizer. She co-edited the collections *Humans of Ballou* and *The Day Tajon Got Shot* from Shout Mouse Press. She volunteers at her local animal rescue and holds an M.F.A. from George Mason University. Find more about her writing, editing, and activism online at www.moonspitpoetry.com.

Photo: Eric Tunell